LAURA OWEN & KORKY PAUL

Winnie AND Wilbur

WINNIE'S
Jokes

OXFORD
UNIVERSITY PRESS

CONTENTS

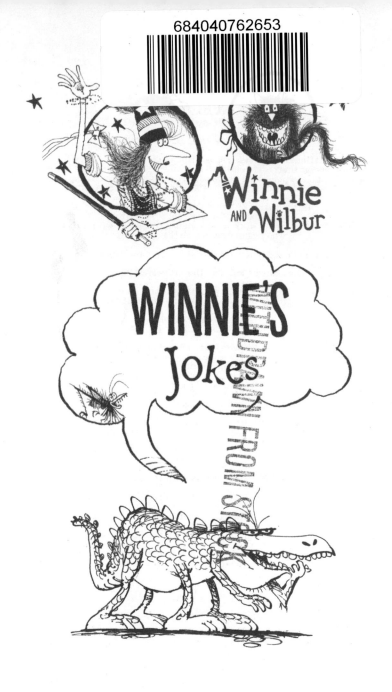

Winnie AND Wilbur

WINNIE'S Jokes

To Mitch Notaras – K.P.

OXFORD
UNIVERSITY PRESS

Great Clarendon Street, Oxford OX2 6DP

Oxford University Press is a department of the University of Oxford.
It furthers the University's objective of excellence in research, scholarship,
and education by publishing worldwide. Oxford is a registered trade mark of
Oxford University Press in the UK and in certain other countries

Compiled and edited by Ron Heapy, with assistance from the pupils of East
Oxford Primary School and Daniel Ron Shaw

First published in 2004
This edition first published in 2016

British Library Cataloguing in Publication Data
Data available

ISBN: 978-0-19-274850-8 (paperback)

2 4 6 8 10 9 7 5 3 1

Printed in Great Britain

Paper used in the production of this book is a natural,
recyclable product made from wood grown in sustainable forests.
The manufacturing process conforms to the environmental
regulations of the country of origin.

WITCHES

Why did Winnie give up tap dancing?

She kept falling into the sink.

What do you call Winnie's sister
Wilma who lives by the sea?

A sandwitch.

Did you hear about the witch
who tried to iron her curtains?

She fell out of the window.

Why does a witch ride on a broom?

Because a vacuum cleaner is too noisy.

How does a witch tell the time?

She wears a witch watch.

Who turns the lights off at Halloween?

The lights witch.

Why couldn't the witch talk on the phone?

She had a frog in her throat.

What sits in a tree with her thumb out?

A witch-hiker.

WITCH 1 What's that on your shoulder?

WITCH 2 That's Tiny.

WITCH 1 Looks like a reptile to me.

WITCH 2 Yes, he's my newt.

Why did the witch cross the road?

It was the chicken's day off.

What do you call a witch with spots?

An itchy witchy.

Why did Winnie keep her wand in the fridge?

She was going through a cold spell.

What do you give a witch at teatime?

A cup and sorcerer.

What do witches use pencil
sharpeners for?

To keep their
hats pointed.

GHOSTS

Where do ghosts buy stamps?

At the ghost office.

Who keeps a watch for ghost ships?

The ghost guard.

What did the phantom
sentry say?

Who ghost there?

What's a ghost's
favourite party game?

Haunt the thimble.

What do you get if
you cross a ghost
with a sailor?

A sea-ghoul.

How do ghosts
fly to America?

By British
Scareways.

WINNIE'S HOUSE

Shall I tell you the joke
about the empty house?

No, there's nothing in it.

How does an intruder get into
Winnie's house?

Intruder windows.

Sounds good.
What kind
of tiles?

Winnie's got
new tiles in
her kitchen.

Reptiles.

BROOMSTICKS

My broom feels very stiff.

What's the matter with it?

It's got broomatism.

My broom was very sad last week.

How do you know?

It went into a corner and swept.

What does an Australian witch ride on?

A broomerang.

How can you tell when witches
are carrying a time-bomb?

You can hear their brooms tick.

Warning on the end of broomsticks:

Don't Fly off the Handle!

Lonely Hearts

Tall, straight, handsome broom,
dark bristles, seeks young, clean,
attractive mop. Likes: night flying
and spring cleaning. No vacuum
cleaners need apply.
Send photo.

ANIMALS

17

My dog's got no nose.

How does he smell?

Terrible.

What do you get if you cross
a sheep with a kangaroo?

A woolly jumper.

How would
you weigh a whale?

At a
whale-weigh
station.

Why don't polar bears wear socks?

Because they like to
walk in their bear feet.

18

MUSIC

What tuba can't you play?

A tuba toothpaste.

Dad: Have you picked up music yet?

Son: Yes, Dad.

Dad: Then help me move this piano.

Why did the opera singer stand on the piano?

So she could reach the high notes.

What shall I sing next?

Do you know 'Loch Lomond'?

Yes.

Then go and jump in it.

WINNIE'S VISITORS

Hello, hello, who's there?

It's the Invisible Man.

Tell him I can't see him.

There's a man at the door with a bill.

Are you sure it isn't a duck
with a hat on?

Who's that at the door?

A man with a drum.

Tell him to beat it.

There's something green and
highly dangerous at the door.

What is it?

A caterpillar with a hand grenade.

MUMMIES

Did you hear about the boy
who had Egyptian flu?

He caught it from his mummy.

Why was the little Egyptian girl confused?

Because her daddy was a mummy.

Why was the mummy so tense?

He was all wound up.

WIZARDS

Which schoolboy wizard
never goes to the barber?

Hairy Potter.

What game do wizard octopuses play?

Squidditch.

Why did the
wizard wear a
pointed hat?

Because he
had a pointed
head.

Why did the wizard wear red,
white, and blue braces?

To keep his trousers up.

Why aren't they making
magic wands any longer?

Because they're long enough already.

What did the wizard say when he
burped while playing football?

Sorry. It was a freak hic.

Why did the wizard keep turning
into Mickey Mouse?

He kept having Disney spells.

Which schoolboy wizard is yellow
and greasy?

Harry Butter.

Did you hear about the wizard who met
a witch in a revolving door?

They've been going round
together ever since.

What do you call a wizard
who makes bowls?

Harry Potter.

Why did the wizard take a fortnight
to make a spell?

It was a slow-motion potion.

Six wizards were standing under
an umbrella. How many got wet?

None of them. It wasn't raining.

What do you call a wizard on his knees?

Neil.

Why do wizards paint the bottoms
of their feet yellow?

So they can hide upside-down
in a bowl of custard.

What happened to the wizard who
couldn't tell putty from toothpaste?

His windows fell out.

What's brown, hairy, wears round
glasses and can do magic?

A coconut disguised as Harry Potter.

FOOTBALL

How did the football pitch end up as a triangle?

Somebody took a corner.

If you have a referee in football and an umpire in tennis, what do you have in bowls?

Goldfish.

26

WINNIE'S RESTAURANT

What's yellow, sharp, and deadly?

Shark-infested custard.

Waiter, waiter! Do you serve children?

Only when we've run out
of everything else, sir.

What kind of soup is this?

It's bean soup, madam.

I don't care what it's been, what is it now?

28

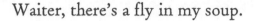

Waiter, there's a fly in my soup.

No, that's the chef, sir. The last customer was a witch doctor.

Waiter, there's a fly in my soup.

Don't worry, madam. That spider on the bread will get him.

Waiter, there's a twig in my soup.

Yes, madam. We've got branches everywhere.

Waiter, there's a beetle in my soup.

I'm terribly sorry, sir. We've run out of flies.

Waiter, these eggs are bad.

Don't blame me, madam.
I only laid the table.

Waiter, I'm in a hurry.
Will my pancake be long?

No, sir, it will be round.

Why are cooks cruel?

They beat eggs, whip cream,
and batter fish.

Which cake is very dangerous?

Attila the Bun.

What's yellow and stupid?

Thick custard.

How do you make a sausage roll?

Push it.

Waiter, I can't eat this soup, it's disgusting. Fetch me the manager.

It's no use, sir.
He won't eat it either.

Waiter, bring me something to eat and make it snappy.

How about a crocodile sandwich, madam?

SKELETONS

MONSTERS

What do sea monsters eat?

Fish and ships.

What's big and green and sits in the corner
all day looking miserable?

The incredible sulk.

What monster lives in your nose?

A bogeyman.

What's a monster's favourite
TV programme?

BeastEnders.

Interviewer: Do you like children?

Monster: Oh, yes, I love children —
boiled, fried, scrambled . . .

What's very large, yellow, lives in
Scotland and has never been seen?

The Loch Ness Canary.

What do monsters make with cars?

Traffic jam.

Which monster runs round
Paris in a plastic bag?

The lunch-pack of Notre Dame.

WILBUR'S FAVOURITES

When is it bad luck to have
a black cat follow you?

When you're a mouse.

What happened to the cat who
swallowed a ball of wool?

She had mittens.

What is an octopus?

An eight-sided cat.

I've lost my cat.

Why don't you put an advertisement
in the newspaper?

Don't be stupid — he can't read.

When should a mouse carry an umbrella?

When it's raining cats and dogs.

What do cats eat for breakfast?

Mice Krispies.

How does a witch's cat stop a DVD?

It pushes the PAWS button.

How can you stop your cat from
miaowing all night in the back garden?

Put him in the front garden.

WINNIE'S LIBRARY

Broken Windows by Eva Brick

Short Skirts by Seymour Leg

The First Bird by Terry Dactyl

The Ghost's Farewell by Fay de Way

The Haunted House by Hugo First

The Unbelievable Truth by R. U. Sure

Out of the Window by Eileen Dover

The Awful Garden by Rosa Weeds

Safe Blowing by Dinah Mite

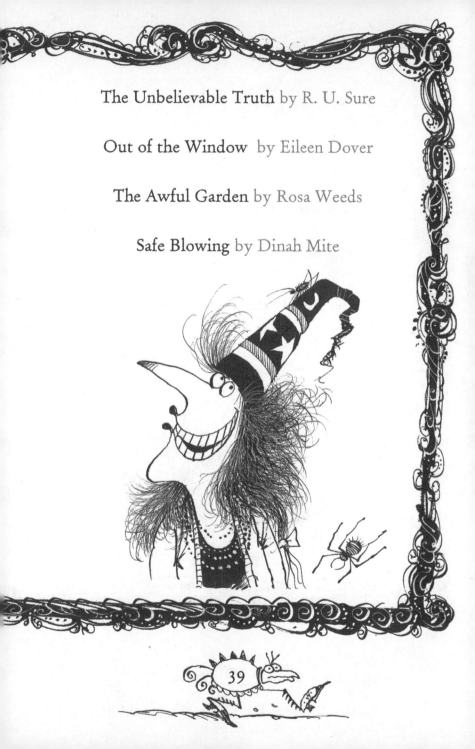

Never Give Up by Percy Vere

Last Day of School by Gladys Friday

Packed Lunches by Sam Widge

Shipwreck! by Mandy Lifeboats

Get Rich Quick by Robin Banks

40

Northern Frights by Philip Skullman

Cookery for Beginners by Egon Chips

Twenty Years in the Saddle by Major Bumsaw

Time for a Cuppa by Lydia Teapot

Down in the Forest by Teresa Green

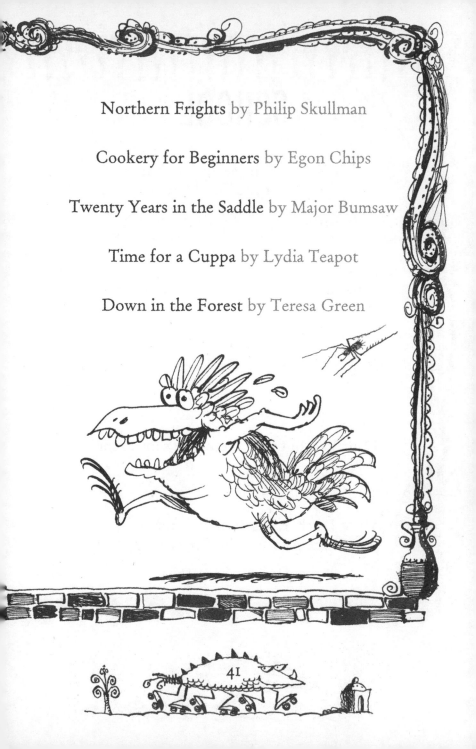

SCHOOL

Teacher: Tell me all you know
about the Dead Sea.

Pupil: I don't know anything.
I didn't even know it was ill.

What do ghouls learn to write in school?

Death sentences.

Dad: Why were you sent home from school?

Son: The boy sitting next to
me was smoking.

Dad: Yes, but why were *you* sent home?

Son: I set fire to him.

Teacher: What came after the
Stone Age and the Bronze Age?

Pupil: The sausage.

Teacher: Who invented fractions?

Pupil: Henry the 1/8th.

Teacher: You're late! You should've been here at 9 o'clock.

Pupil: Why, miss? What happened?

Teacher: If I had ten pineapples in one hand, and six in the other, what would I have?

Pupil: Very big hands, miss.

43

What sea creature is good at maths?

An octoplus.

Mother: What did you learn on your
first day at school?

Child: Not much.
I have to go back tomorrow.

A Short School Test

1. Which is the odd one out?
Dog Dog Dog Wilbur Dog

2. Add 481 and 845. Double it.
Multiply it by 37 and divide it by 9.
Close your eyes.
Dark, isn't it?

WINNIE'S SALE

Twenty-five bottles of
invisible ink. You can't
see it, but trust me.

Fourteen budgies.
All going cheep.

Full suit of armour.
Good for haunting castles.
Suitable for gentleman
ghost. Free oil can.

Bulldog for sale. Will eat
anything. Especially fond
of children.

Parachute for sale.
No strings attached.

45

WEREWOLVES

How do you know that a werewolf's been in the fridge?

There are pawprints in the butter.

What happened to the werewolf that fell into the washing machine?

It became a wash-n-werewolf.

I used to be a werewolf but I'm all right noooooooowwwwww.

KNOCK KNOCK

Knock Knock

Who's there?

A man who can't reach the doorbell

Knock Knock

Who's there?

Sadie

Sadie who?

Sadie magic words.

Knock Knock

Who's there?

Arfer

Arfer who?

Arfer got.

Knock Knock

Who's there?

Madge

Madge who?

Madge E. Quand.

Knock Knock

Who's there?

Wand

Wand who?

Wand to come in.

FISH

How can you tell that fish are musical?

Send for the piano tuna.

What lies at the bottom of the sea and is very dangerous?

Billy the Squid.

Which fish terrorizes other fish?

Jack the Kipper.

What's the best way to communicate with a fish?

Drop it a line.

ELEPHANTS

What's the difference between an
African elephant and an Indian elephant?

About 3000 miles.

What do you call a man with an
elephant on his head?

Squashed.

What's the difference between
an elephant and a biscuit?

You can't dip an elephant in your tea.

What do you call an elephant that flies?

A jumbo jet.

Hickory, Dickory, Dock.
The elephant ran up the clock.
The clock is now being repaired.

WINNIE'S SHOPPING LIST

Hamsterburgers
Hot frogs
KFC (Krispy Fried Cockroaches)
Mice Cream
Spooketti
Hot cross bunnies
Scream of tomato soup
Ghoulash
Dreaded Wheat
Prickled onions
Mouse-aka (made with real mouse)

DINOSAURS

What should you do if you find
a dinosaur in your bed?

Sleep somewhere else.

How do you ask a dinosaur to dinner?

Tea, Rex?

Why did the dinosaur cross the road?

Chickens hadn't been invented yet.

What do you get when dinosaurs
crash their cars?

Tyrannosaurus wrecks.

WINNIE'S COMPUTER

There's a spider in Winnie's computer.

What's he doing?

He's set up his own website.

What do computers have for lunch?

Spam and chips.

Why does Dracula like computers?

Because they've got so many bytes in them.

Why did the footballer kick his computer?

He wanted to boot up the system.

HERE IS THE NEWS

The Eddystone lighthouse
has just been stolen.
The police are anxious
to interview a man
last seen boarding
a 52 bus carrying
a long, brown paper parcel.

DOCTOR, DOCTOR

Doctor, doctor, my wooden leg
is giving me a lot of pain.

Why's that?

My wife keeps hitting me on the head with it.

Doctor, doctor,
I keep thinking I'm a pack of cards.

Sit down, I'll deal with you later.

Doctor, doctor,
I think I'm a pair of curtains.

Well, pull yourself together.

Doctor, doctor,
I've lost my memory.

When did it happen?

When did what happen?

Doctor, doctor, I keep thinking I'm a spoon.

Well, sit there and don't stir.

Come down off the ceiling and we'll talk about it.

Doctor, doctor, I think I'm a fly.

Doctor, doctor, I think I'm shrinking.

Well, you'll just have to be a little patient.

Doctor, doctor, I think I need glasses.

You certainly do. This is a fish and chip shop.

VAMPIRES

What did the vampire
say to his victim?
Your neck's
on my list.

What's Dracula's
favourite song?
Fangs for the
Memory.

Where does Dracula
stay when he goes
to New York?
In the Vampire
State Building.

What do you call
a blood-drinking
sheep?
A lambpire.

WINNIE'S RAGBAG OF JOKES

Help, help! I've swallowed a bone.

Are you choking?

No, I'm serious.

What do you get if you put your auntie in the fridge?

Aunti-freeze.

Who's the boss of the hankies?

The hankie chief.

Where do hangmen look for jobs?

In the noosepaper.

What's a hangman's favourite TV programme?

Noose at Ten.

Wilma's broken my doll.

How did she do that?

I hit her with it.

What would you do with a sick wasp?

Take it to a waspital.

What do you get if you jump in the River Nile?

Wet.

Have you seen an abominable snowman?

Not yeti.

What do you call two corpses in a belfry?

Dead ringers.

Can a man marry his widow's sister?

No, he'd have to be dead
to have a widow.

How many dead people
are buried in that cemetery?

All of them.

What lies at the bottom of
the sea and whimpers?

A nervous wreck.

What do you
do if the M6 is
closed?

Drive up the
M3 twice.

AND FINALLY...